A Kid's Guide to Making Friends

A Children's Book about Social Skills

by

Joy Wilt

Illustrated by Ernie Hergenroeder

Educational Products Division
Word, Incorporated
Waco, Texas

Author

JOY WILT is creator and director of Children's Ministries, an organization that provides resources "for people who care about children"—speakers, workshops, demonstrations, consulting services, and training institutes. A certified elementary school teacher, administrator, and early childhood specialist, Joy is also consultant to and professor in the master's degree program in children's ministries for Fuller Theological Seminary. Joy is a graduate of LaVerne College, LaVerne, California (B.A. in Biological Science), and Pacific Oaks College, Pasadena, California (M.A. in Human Development). She is author of three books, *Happily Ever After, An Uncomplicated Guide to Becoming a Superparent*, and *Taming the Big Bad Wolves*, as well as the popular *Can-Make-And-Do Books*. Joy's commitment "never to forget what it feels like to be a child" permeates the many innovative programs she has developed and her work as lecturer, consultant, writer, and—not least—mother of two children, Christopher and Lisa.

Artist

ERNIE HERGENROEDER is founder and owner of Hergie & Associates (a visual communications studio and advertising agency). With the establishment of this company in 1975, "Hergie" and his wife, Faith, settled in San Jose with their four children, Lynn, Kathy, Stephen, and Beth. Active in community and church affairs, Hergie is involved in presenting creative workshops for teachers, ministers, and others who wish to understand the techniques of communicating visually. He also lectures in high schools to encourage young artists toward a career in commercial art. Hergie serves as a consultant to organizations such as the Police Athletic League (PAL), Girl Scouts, and religious and secular corporations. His ultimate goal is to touch the hearts of kids (8 to 80) all over the world—visually!

Contents

Introduction

A Kid's Guide to Making Friends is one of a series of books. The complete set is called *Ready-Set-Grow!*

A Kid's Guide to Making Friends deals with friendship, and can be used by itself or as a part of a program that utilizes all of the *Ready-Set-Grow!* books.

A Kid's Guide to Making Friends is specifically designed so that children can either read the book themselves or have it read to them. This can be done at home, church, or school. When reading to children, it is not necessary to complete the book at one sitting. Concern should be given to the attention span of the individual child and his or her comprehension of the subject matter.

A Kid's Guide to Making Friends is designed to involve the child in the concepts that are being taught. This is done by simply and carefully explaining each concept and then asking questions that invite a response from the child. It is hoped that by answering the questions the child will personalize the concept and, thus, integrate it into his or her thinking.

How a person relates to other people is crucial to what he or she is and what he or she will become. Healthy, productive friendships are essential for a normal, happy life.

A Kid's Guide to Making Friends explains to the child what a friendship is, how to start a friendship, and how to make a friendship grow. The book advocates that God has given us all basic guidelines for making and keeping friends. These are:

make the other person feel special,

make the other person feel important, and

listen carefully to the other person.

Friendships are important to a child's happiness and emotional development. Children need opportunities to develop and express loyalty to chosen friends. The closeness, the sharing, and the feeling of belonging with one's own contemporaries are important factors in survival and growth.

A Kid's Guide to Making Friends is designed to teach the child methods of friendship. The child will learn the rule: to be a friend is to have a friend. This book is also designed to teach a child that everything God does has a purpose and fits into a total plan. "Making and keeping friends" is a part of God's plan for every human being. Children who grow up believing this will be better equipped to live healthy, exciting lives.

A Kid's Guide to Making Friends

God created you a person, and because you are one . . .

you need to have friends.

People were created by God to need each other.

Every person needs to have friends.

Chapter 1

What Is a Friend?

A friend is someone who likes you.

A friend is someone you like.

Not all friends are alike. There are different kinds of friends.

One kind of friend is called an acquaintance.

Acquaintances seldom spend time together.

Acquaintances may like each other,
but they do not know each other very well.

17

Usually every person has many acquaintances.

Having many acquaintances helps make life interesting.

Another kind of friend is called a playmate.

Playmates see each other often.

Playmates like playing together.

Usually every person has several playmates.

Having several playmates helps make life fun and enjoyable.

A third kind of friend is called a best friend.

Most best friends live close together and are able to
see each other quite often.

A few best friends do not live close together and are unable to see each other very often.

But whether best friends live close together or far apart . . .

they love each other. **27**

Best friends show their love for each other by spending time together whenever they can.

They show their love by sharing their things with each other.

Best friends show their love by helping each other whenever they can.

They respect each other.

Best friends respect each other's body.

They respect each other's thoughts and feelings. **33**

Best friends respect each other's things.

34

They trust each other.

Best friends can depend on each other.

They are honest with each other, and they keep their promises.

37

Best friends are unselfish, and they are fair with each other.

They like to do things together.

39

Best friends enjoy being around each other.

A best friend is one of the best things a person can have. **41**

So . . . all kinds of friends are important.

Every person needs to have

      acquaintances,
      playmates, and
      at least one best friend.

Do you have any acquaintances?

What are their names?

_____

_____

_____

_____

_____

Do you have any playmates?

Who are some of your playmates, and what are the things you like doing most when you are together?

PLAYMATE CHART

Playmate's Name	Favorite Activity

Do you have any best friends?

If you do, what are their names?

_____

_____

Most people do not have more than one or two best friends. This is because best friends are hard to find, and friendships between best friends require a lot of hard work.

Chapter 2

How to Make a Friend

Before a person makes a friend, he or she needs to know these two things.

Every human being is special.

Every human being is important.

There are several things a person needs to do when making a friend. What are these things?

The first thing to do when making a friend is to think of the other person as being special.

MELISSA IS VERY SPECIAL. SHE CAN DO SO MANY THINGS WELL, ESPECIALLY PAINTING. Ooooo...

Do everything you can to make the other person feel special.

Think of a person you are friends with or would like to be friends with.

Think about how this person looks, acts, thinks, and feels.

List the things that make this person special.

_____

_____

_____

How could you make this person feel special?

What could you say?

_____

What could you do?

_____

The second thing to do when making a friend is to think of the other person as being important.

Think of a person you are friends with or would like to be friends with.

Think about how this person treats other people, how he or she helps them, and what he or she does to make things better.

List the things that make this person important to you.

_____

_____

_____

How could you make this person feel important?

What could you say?

_____

What could you do?

_____

The third thing to do when making a friend is to show the other person that you are interested in him or her.

Do everything you can to make the other person feel that you are interested in him or her.

Think of a person you are friends with or would like to be friends with.

Think about this person's family and friends, where he or she lives, where he or she goes to church and school, what special talents he or she has, and what his or her hobbies are.

List the things about this person that you can show an interest in.

_____

_____

_____

How could you make this person feel that you are interested in him or her?

What could you say?

_____

What could you do?

_____

The fourth thing to do when making a friend is to remember
that a person's name is very important.

Call the person by his or her name as often as you can.

Remember these things about people's names.

First names — Most people (except for some grown-ups) like to be called by their first names.

Middle names — It's sometimes fun to know a person's middle name. Although many people like to be called by their middle names, a lot of people do not.

Last names — Knowing a person's last name is important, especially if there are several people in your group of acquaintances, playmates, and friends who have the same first name. Some people like to be called by their last names, but don't do it unless they like it.

Nicknames — A nickname is OK as long as the person who is being called by the nickname likes it. Never call a person by a nickname that he or she does not like.

How well do you know the names of your friends?
Can you fill out this name chart?

FIRST NAME	MIDDLE NAME	LAST NAME	NICKNAME

The fifth thing to do when making a friend is to
be a good listener.

Listen carefully to the other person and encourage
him or her to talk about himself or herself. **67**

How well do you listen?

Think of the last conversation you had with a friend.

What was the conversation about?

_____

How much of what your friend said do you remember?

_____

Who talked the most?

_____

What can you do to get another person to talk about himself or herself?

What are some questions you could ask?

_____

_____

_____

The sixth thing to do when making a friend is to talk to the other person about things that interest him or her.

If the other person is not interested in what you are saying, talk about something else.

Think of a person you are friends with or would like to be friends with.

List some of the things this person would be interested in talking about.

_____

_____

_____

Remember that most people are interested in themselves and what they like to do.

Knowing this, how could you make the other person feel that you are interested in talking with him or her?

What could you say?

_____

What could you do?

_____

Remember this.

In order to make a friend, you need to know these two things.

Every human being is special.

Every human being is important.

In order to make a friend, you also need to do these things.

Make the other person feel special.

Make the other person feel important.

Make the other person feel that you are interested in him or her.

Call the other person by his or her name as often as you can.

Listen carefully to the other person.

Talk to the other person about things that interest him or her.

How well can you remember about making a friend?

What are the two things you need to know about people?
What are the six things you need to do in order to make a friend?

Chapter 3

How to Keep a Friend

Before a person can keep a friend, he or she needs to know these three things.

No one is perfect. Everyone needs to become a better person.

A person improves best when he or she is allowed to develop in his or her own way and at his or her own pace.

Every person has something valuable and important to give other people.

There are several things a person needs to do in order to keep a friend. What are these things?

The first thing to do in order to keep a friend is to accept the other person the way he or she is.

Don't force the other person to change or be different from the way he or she is.

81

Pretend that the person on the next page is talking to you.

How would you feel?

What would you think?

Would you want this person to be your friend?

Why or why not?

83

The second thing to do in order to keep a friend is to appreciate the other person.

Tell the other person you think well of him or her, and praise him or her whenever you can.

Think of a person you are friends with. List things about that friend you appreciate.

_____

_____

Does that friend know you appreciate him or her?

Have you told him or her?

Does anyone appreciate you?

How do you feel when someone appreciates you?

The third thing to do in order to keep a friend is to encourage the other person.

YOU'RE DOING GREAT, PETE!

Tell the other person that he or she is doing OK, and give him or her courage, hope, and confidence to keep trying.

Think of a person you are friends with.

Have you ever encouraged that friend?

When was the last time you encouraged him or her?

_____

How did you encourage him or her?

_____

Has anyone ever encouraged you?

How do you feel when someone encourages you?

_____

The fourth thing to do in order to keep a friend is to put yourself in the other person's place.

Try to understand how the other person thinks and feels, and respect his or her thoughts and feelings.

Think of a person you are friends with.

Has that friend ever gotten hurt while you were playing with him or her?

How did he or she feel?

_____

What did you do?

_____

Has that friend ever lost or broken something that was important to him or her?

How did he or she feel?

_____

What did you do?

_____

Has that friend ever gotten in trouble?

How did he or she feel?

_____

What did you do?

_____

Has that friend ever gotten angry?
What made him or her angry?

_____

What did you do?

_____

The fifth thing to do in order to keep a friend is don't nag at or argue with the other person.

JOEY'S LATE AGAIN, BUT I'M NOT GOING TO NAG HIM ABOUT IT, BECAUSE THAT WON'T HELP ANY. HE PROBABLY FEELS BAD ENOUGH AS IT IS!

Try to solve your problems without nagging and arguing.

Think of a person you are friends with.

Does that friend ever nag at you?

How does this make you feel?

_____

Do you ever nag at that friend?

How do you think this makes him or her feel?

_____

When was the last time you had an argument with that friend?

_____

What was the argument about?

_____

How did the argument make you feel?

_____

The sixth thing to do in order to keep a friend
is to tell the other person whenever you make
a mistake or do something wrong that
affects him or her.

If what you have done has hurt the other person, admit what you did, tell the other person that you are sorry, and ask him or her to forgive you. **101**

When was the last time you made a mistake or did something wrong that affected a friend?

_____

What was your mistake, or what did you do wrong?

_____

How did you feel after your mistake or wrongdoing?

_____

What did you do?

_____

The seventh thing to do in order to keep a friend is to try to make the other person feel better when he or she makes a mistake or does something wrong.

I FORGIVE YOU, PETE. I KNOW YOU DIDN'T BREAK MY PLANE ON PURPOSE.

Do your best to forgive the other person and make him or her feel
at ease about the mistake or wrongdoing.

Think of a person you are friends with.

When was the last time that friend made a mistake or did something wrong that you knew about?

_____

What was his or her mistake, or what did he or she do wrong?

_____

How do you think that friend felt after his or her mistake or wrongdoing?

_____

What did he or she do?

_____

How did you react?

_____

What did you do to make that friend feel better?

_____

The eighth thing to do in order to keep a friend is to do something special once in a while to show you like the other person.

Remind the other person that you like him or her by making or doing something for him or her.

Think of a person you are friends with.

When was the last time you did something special for that friend?

_____

What did you do?

_____

How do you think this made him or her feel?

_____

How did you feel?

_____

When was the last time someone did something special for you?

_____

What did that person do?

_____

How did this make you feel?

_____

How do you think he or she felt?

_____

Remember this.

In order to keep a friend, you need to know these three things.

No one is perfect. Everyone needs to become a better person.

A person improves best when he or she is allowed to develop in his or her own way and at his or her own pace.

Every person has something valuable and important to give other people.

In order to keep a friend, you also need to do these things.

Accept the other person.

Appreciate the other person.

Encourage the other person.

Put yourself in the other person's place.

Don't nag at or argue with the other person.

Tell the other person whenever you make a mistake or do something wrong.

Try to make the other person feel better about his or her mistakes and wrongdoings.

Do something special to show you like the other person.

How well can you remember about keeping a friend?

What are the three things you need to know about people?

What are the eight things you need to do in order to keep a friend?

Conclusion

Acquaintances.

Playmates.

Best friends.

These are the three kinds of friends that are extremely important for you to have.

Friends don't just happen. It takes work to make acquaintances, playmates, and best friends.

But remember that the good things you do to make
a friend will always be worthwhile because . . .

A friend makes life more interesting.

A friend can bring you joy and happiness.

A friend can comfort you when you are feeling sad.

So the things you do to make friends . . .

Make the other person feel special.

Make the other person feel important.

Make the other person feel that you are interested in him or her.

Call the other person by his or her name as often as you can.

Listen carefully to the other person.

Talk to the other person about things that interest him or her.

Accept the other person.

Appreciate the other person.

Encourage the other person.

Put yourself in the other person's place.

Don't nag at or argue with the other person.

Tell the other person whenever you make a mistake or do something wrong.

Try to make the other person feel better about his or her mistakes and wrongdoings.

Do something special to show you like the other person.

are all worthwhile because . . .

Friends are one of the best things . . .

a person can ever have.